WHEN

Was the first robot made?

Om KIDZ
An imprint of Om Books International

Contents

When is a machine called a robot?

A machine is called a robot when it can carry out a series of complex actions automatically. A robot is programmable by a computer and guided by an external control device. It can only perform tasks that engineers program into its computer. Each robot is designed differently based on the job it does.

Find out

What was the clock jack?

Pocket fact

The Hero of Alexandria wrote a book *Automata*. It is a collection of different devices which could have been used in temples thousands of years ago.

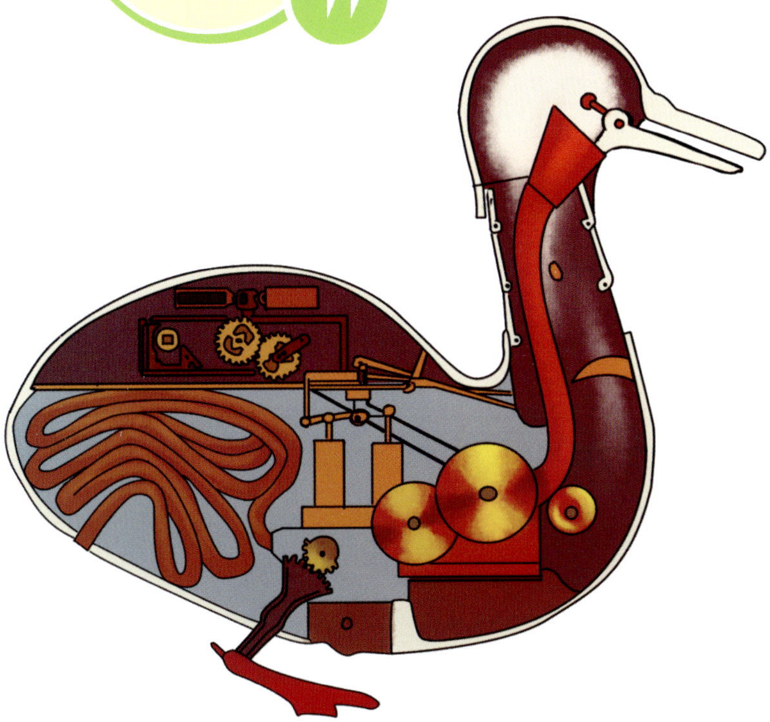

When were robot-like creatures first observed?

Long ago in the 18th century! Robot-like miniature devices were popular as toys for the rich. These looked and moved like small animals or humans. A famous creation of this time was a mechanical device "The Duck" created by Jacques de Vaucanson. It had wings with over four hundred moving parts. The duck could flap its wings, eat and even digest grain! Vaucanson also created an automated human figure that played the flute.

When was the Steam Man invented?

In 1868! The Steam Man was a steam-powered robot invented by Zadoc P. Dederick. He developed a humanoid steam-powered robot that could tow a cart. The device, which was granted a patent on March 24, 1868, worked by use of a set of levers and cranks that were connected to a boiler and steam-powered pistons. It was used to pull wheeled carts!

Pocket fact

A fictional robot called the Electric Man was made by the protagonist Frank Reade Jr. of a popular series of dime novels published in the late 1800s.

Find out

What does the word robot mean?

When was the term robot first used?

In 1921! The term "robot" was first used in a play written by the Czech writer Karel Capek. The play was called "R.U.R." or "Rossum's Universal Robots". In this play, a man creates a robot to replace him but later the robot kills the man!

When was the human-like robot ELEKTRO introduced?

In 1939! The human-like robot ELEKTRO was created by the Westinghouse Electric Corporation in Mansfield between the years 1937-1938. It could walk, talk, smoke and had voice control. It was first introduced at the 1939 world's fair. ELEKTRO was seven-feet tall and weighed 265 pounds. It could say around 700 words by producing a low dull sound from a 78 rpm record player hidden behind a curtain.

Pocket fact

Sparko!
Sparko was a robot dog that joined ELEKTRO at the 1940 World's Fair. It could both bark and sit on command.

Find out

Who is called the father of robotics?

Robotics

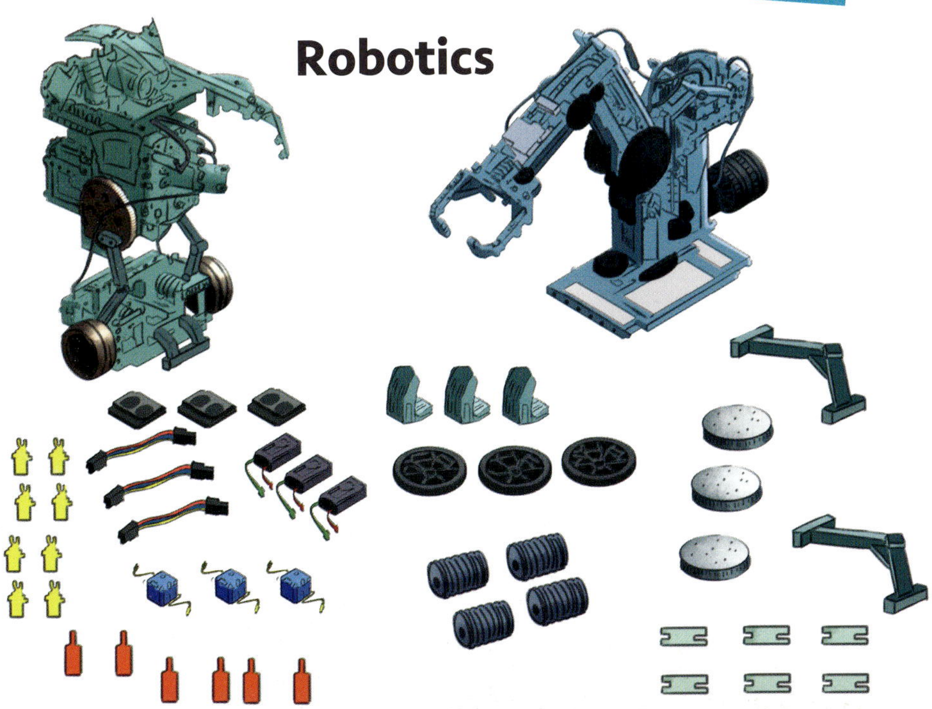

When was the word "robotics" first used?

In 1941! The word 'robotics' was first used by the science writer Isaac Asimov. It was used to describe the technology of robots. Today robotics is said to be the study and use of robots. Asimov also predicted that robotics will be a powerful industry in the future.

When was the first modern robot invented?

In 1954! The first truly programmable robot was invented by an American engineer Geroge Devol. It was called the UNIMATE, short form for "Universal Automation". It was a robotic arm that could repeat a sequence of actions and was used in industries.

Find out

What was the name of the world's first robot manufacturing called?

Pocket fact

4000 pounds!

The UNIMATE robot weighed 4000 pounds. It was controlled by vacuum tubes used as digital switches.

When did the world's first robot go to work?

In 1961! The world's first robot that went to work was the robotic arm, UNIMATE. It was introduced by George Devol in a die-casting factory of General Motors in New Jersey. Its job was to remove and stack hot metal parts from a die-casting machine and weld these parts on auto bodies. The robot was quite helpful to factory workers who could be poisoned by exhaust gas or lose a limb if they were not careful.

When was the first robotic pet created?

The first robotic pet was invented by the Sony Company (Japan) in 1999. It was a robotic dog and was called AIBO. It had a beagle-like appearance and could interact with people. AIBO is a series of robotic pets manufactured by Sony. Though most models resemble dogs, there are other pets like lion cubs and space explorers.

Find out

What does the word AIBO mean?

Pocket fact

Tweet Tweet!
Robonaut sent its first tweet on 26 July 2010.

When would organizations other than NASA benefit from Robonaut?

In just a few years from now! NASA's partner, General Motors, is working towards using R2 to make its cars safer. It also hopes to use lessons drawn from R2 to make a safer work environment.

When was the El-E fetch robot invented?

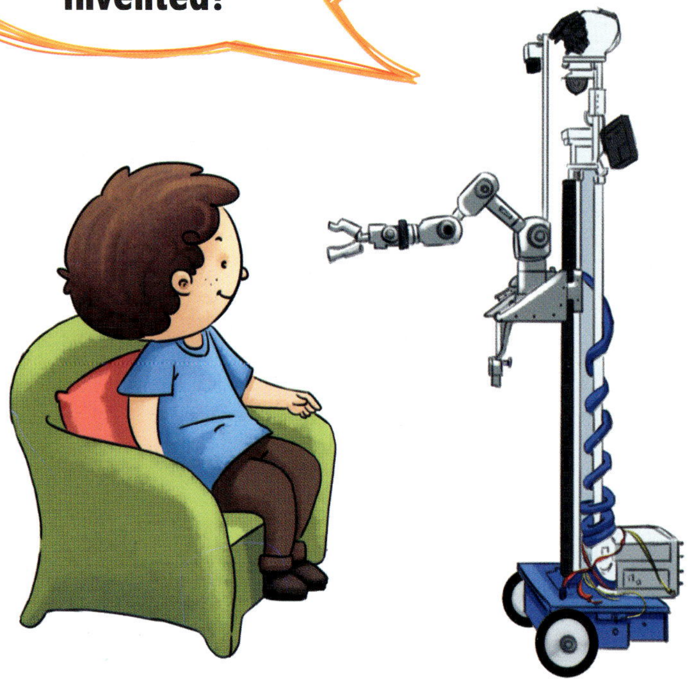

In 2008! The El-E Fetch is a robot that helps people who have trouble getting around. It is about 5.7 feet tall and has two camera eyes. El-E Fetch is automated and understands commands using a simple laser pointer. When you point the laser at any object around, the robot will run across the room, pick it up and give it to you. It can also speak, wash dishes and even clean up the entire house!

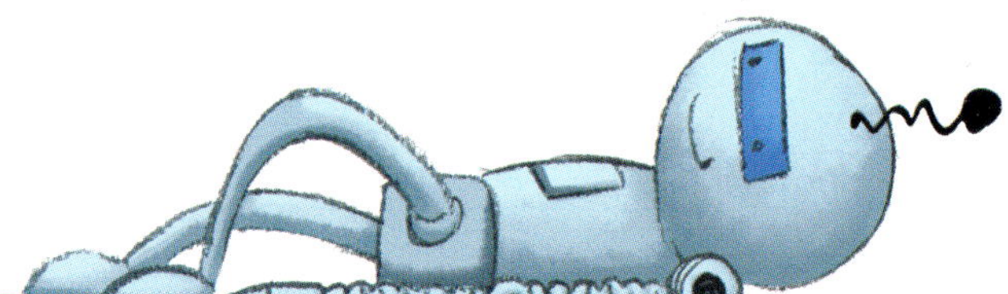

Pocket fact

The Kuratas is said to be the world's first giant robot. It was demonstrated at the Wonder Festival in Japan.

Find out

What is the full form of El-E in the name of El-E Fetch robot?

When was the world's biggest robot created?

In 2012! The world's biggest robot is the Kuratas developed by artist Kogoro Kurata and roboticist Wataru Yoshizaki in Japan. It is 4 metres high, weighs approximately 4,500 kgs and has four wheels. It can be crewed by one person. The operator sits on a seat inside the robot and controls it using the device in front of him. The Kuratas can also be controlled by a remote control.

When was the QRIO robot created?

In 2003! The QRIO was a bipedal humanoid robot developed by the Sony Company. It was 2 feet tall and weighed 7.3 kg. It was created to follow up on the success of Sony's AIBO entertainment robot. QRIO robot could recognize the voice and face. This enabled it to remember people and also their likes and dislikes!

Find out

What is the full form of ASIMO?

Pocket fact

The QRIO was originally called the Sony Dream Robot.
The full form of QRIO is Quest for CuRIOsity.

When was the ASIMO robot invented?

In 2000! The ASIMO is the world's most advanced humanoid robot and was created by the Honda Motor Company. It is 4 feet 3 inches tall. ASIMO can walk on its own, climb stairs, recognize its user's voice, face and name. It can also turn on lights, open doors, carry things, and even read emails!

When was the first biped robot created?

In 1973! The first biped robot was called the Wabot-1. It was created by Waseda University, Japan. It could walk with its lower limbs, and gripped and transported objects with hands. Wabot-1 could also measure distances and directions to objects using external receptors, artificial eyes and ears.

Pocket fact

A biped robot is the one that can walk on two legs just as we do.

Find out

Where did the HelpMate robot first went to work?

When was the HelpMate robot invented?

In 1984! The HelpMate is a mobile robot developed by Joseph Frederick Engelberger for hospitals and nursing homes. It can navigate throughout a hospital by following a map stored in its memory. HelpMate can also carry medical supplies, records and lab samples and deliver them to different hospital departments.

When were rover robots sent to Mars?

In 2003! NASA launched twin robotic rovers called Spirit and Sojourner as part of their mission to explore Mars. The Sojourner is 6 inches long, 19 inches wide, and 12 inches tall. The Spirit is 7.5 feet long, 5 feet wide and 5 feet tall. The Sojourner took 550 photographs and did some research on a rock named Yogi.

Find out

What is the other name of the rover Spirit?

Pocket fact

The first model of a robonaut was called Robonaut 1 or R1.
It head, two eyes, two arms and two five-digit hands.

When was the R2 robot sent to space?

R2 is a robonaut invented by NASA. It is a human-like robot and can handle a wide range of tools. It has a computer in its belly and camera sensors in its head. These camera sensors help it to see. The R2 was sent aboard the International Space Station in 2011 and hopes to take over repetitive and dangerous tasks on the International Space Station.

When was the world's smallest and lightest robot helicopter invented?

In 2003! The world's smallest and lightest robot helicopter model is the Micro Flying Robot. It was developed by Seiko Epson to explore the possible use of micro robots. It has two microprocessors, Bluetooth, a gyro-sensor and image sensor. The robot is powered by an external battery through a power cable and thus cannot fly high.

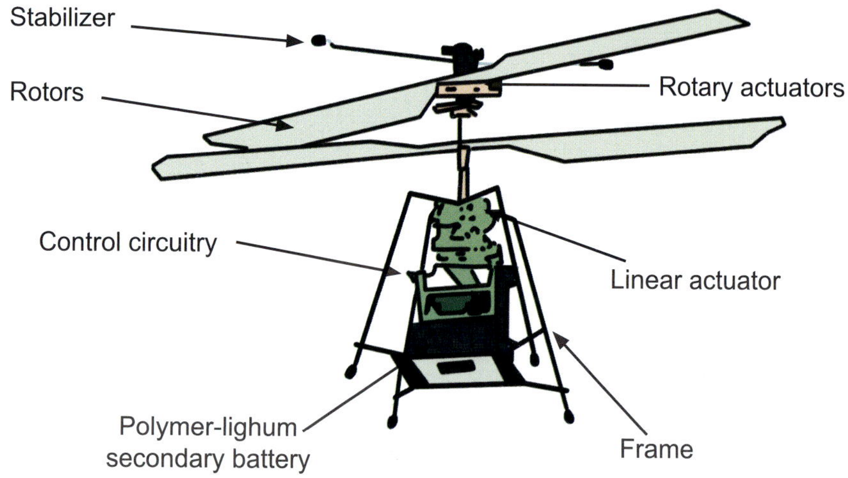

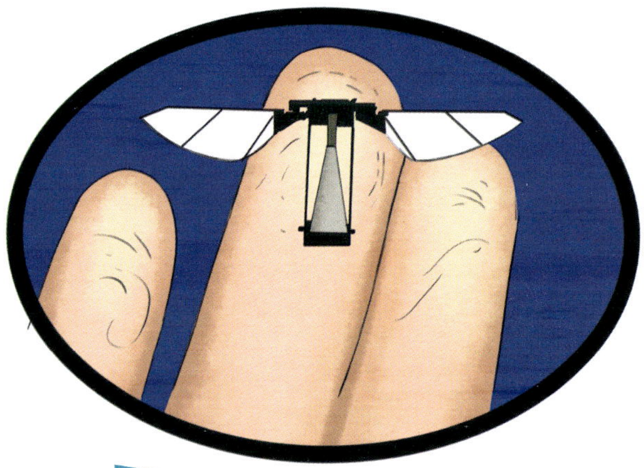

Find out

Which is the world's smallest microrobot?

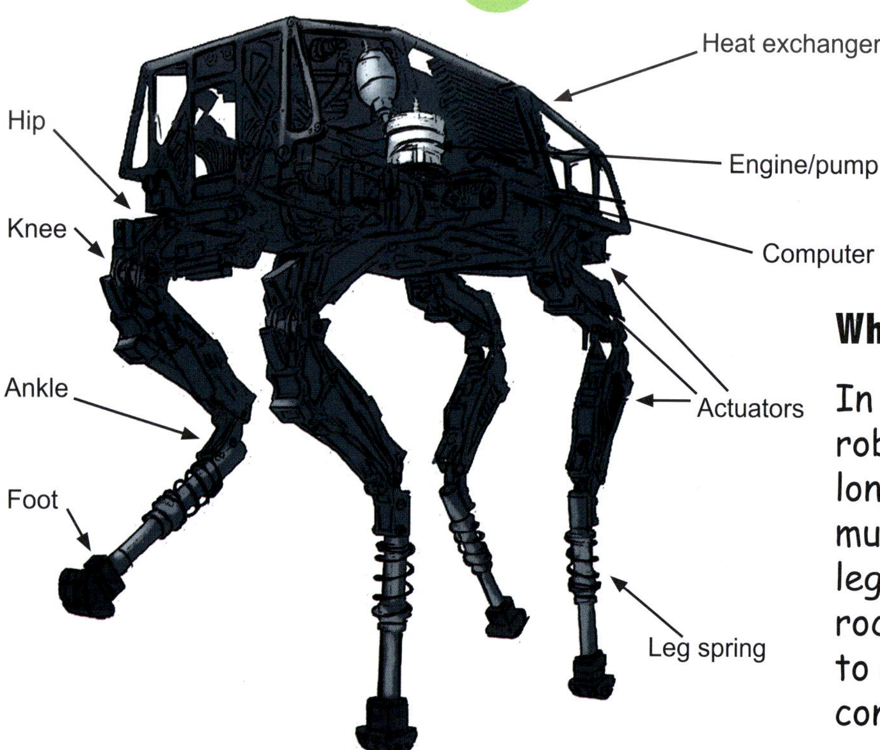

Pocket fact

The Big Dog can walk in snow and water, climb muddy hiking trails, and carry up to 150kg loads.

When was the Big Dog robot invented?

In 2005! The Big Dog is a four-legged military robot created by Boston Dynamics. It is 3 feet long and 2.5 feet tall about the size of a small mule. It doesn't have wheels, instead uses its legs to follow a person and move safely around rocks and trees. The Big Dog was invented to accompany soldiers in rough lands where conventional vehicles cannot be used.

When was the ACTUV robot ship invented?

In 2010! The ACTUV is a robot ship invented by the US Navy. It is designed to track submarines for up to 90 days at sea. It is in constant contact with other ships and aircraft through a satellite link. If there's no threat, a sailor can order the robot to go back on patrol.

Pocket fact

The Actroid robot can talk to a group of people and also handle if someone interrupts it while talking.

Find out

What is a female Android robot called?

When was the Actroid robot created?

The Actroid is a humanoid robot created by Osaka University, Japan. Its skin is made of silicone and looks like a young Japanese child. Actroid has speech recognition software. It can copy basic human functions and can talk and blink. It was introduced at the 2003 International Robot Exhibition, Tokyo.

When was the Zeno robot invented?

In 2007! Zeno is a humanoid robot boy developed by a team from Imperial College London to interact with children who have autism. It is 17 inches tall and weighs 4.5 pounds. Its prototype was displayed at the 2007 Wired Nextfest. Zeno is said to be an intelligent "conversational robot" that will teach autistic children how to understand and convey their emotions.

Pocket fact

Zeno teaches in a fun way. It plays games, shows pictures, tells stories and asks the children to describe what they see!!

Find out

How many kinds of robots are there?

When does a robot get tired?

Never! A robot is a machine that can be designed for working continuously. It doesn't need food and water like humans. It can work without getting bored and tired. All we need to make sure is to provide the robot with a correct set of instructions and power it with an electric outlet or battery so that they can work efficiently.

When can a robot stop working?

When you run a robot beyond its operation time! Robots are machines that should be inspected and maintained regularly. Most robots have a fixed period of operating time. Robots may stop working after those fixed hours. They also don't work when there is cable damage, the software is corrupt or they lose their ability to smoothly perform actions repeatedly.

Pocket fact

Most industry robots have a 3,840 hour period of operating time.

Find out

What should we do to prevent robot malfunctions?

When does a robot malfunction?

There are many reasons! A robotic malfunction occurs when it behaves differently- smashing and destroying things. This can occur due to a lot of reasons like errors in program, control panels, a failure in the power source or even wrong installation of its equipment.

Index